OUR SOUTHERN NEIGHBOR MEXICO

THE FESTIVALS OF MEXICO

COLLEEN MADONNA FLOOD WILLIAMS

Festival decorations hang in a doorway in a Mexican town. The people of Mexico carefully plan and prepare for the rituals of various festivals, since the celebrations are a significant and meaningful part of Mexican culture.

THE FESTIVALS OF MEXICO

COLLEEN MADONNA FLOOD WILLIAMS

Mason Crest Publishers
Philadelphia

Mason Crest Publishers
370 Reed Road
Broomall PA 19008
www.masoncrest.com

First printing

1 3 5 7 9 8 6 4 2

Library of Congress Cataloging-in-Publication Data on file at the Library of Congress

Williams, Colleen Madonna Flood.
The Festivals of Mexico / by Colleen Madonna Flood Williams.
    p.   cm.   — (Mexico: our southern neighbor)
Includes bibliographical references and index.
Summary: Presents Mexico's many festivals and holidays, which
may be religious, national, local, or personal, and describes how
they are celebrated.
ISBN 1-59084-078-X (hc)
1. Festivals—Mexico—Juvenile literature. 2. Mexico—Social life
and customs—Juvenile literature. [1. Festivals—Mexico. 2.
Holidays—Mexico. 3. Mexico—Social life and customs.] I. Title.
II. Series.
GT4814.A2 W53 2002
394.26972—dc21

       2001052214

TABLE OF CONTENTS

OUR
SOUTHERN NEIGHBOR
MEXICO

Roger E. Hernández
Senior Consulting Editor

INTRODUCTION

Mexico is a country in the midst of great change. And what happens in Mexico will have an important impact on the United States, its neighbor to the north.

These changes are being put in place by President Vicente Fox, who was elected in 2000. For the previous 71 years, power had been held by presidents from one single party, known in Spanish as *Partido Revolucionario Institucional* (Institutional Revolutionary Party, or PRI). Some of those presidents have been accused of corruption. President Fox, from a different party called *Partido de Acción Nacional* (National Action Party, or PAN), says he wants to eliminate that corruption. He also wants to have a friendlier relationship with the United States, and for American businesses to increase trade with Mexico. That will create more jobs, he says, and decrease poverty—which in turn will mean fewer Mexicans will find themselves forced to emigrate in search of a better life.

But it would be wrong to think of Mexico as nothing more than a poor country. Mexico has given the world some of its greatest artists and writers. Carlos Fuentes is considered one of the greatest living novelists, and poet-essayist Octavio Paz was awarded the Nobel Prize for Literature in 1990, the most prestigious honor a writer can win. Painters such as Diego Rivera and José Clemente Orozco specialized in murals, huge paintings done on walls that tell of the history of the nation. Another famous Mexican painter, Rufino Tamayo, blended the "cubist" style of modern European painters like Picasso with native folk themes.

Tamayo's paintings in many ways symbolize what Mexico is: A blend of the culture of Europe (more specifically, its Spanish version) and the indigenous cultures that predated the arrival of Columbus.

Those cultures were thriving even 3,000 years ago, when the Olmec people built imposing monuments that survive to this day in what are now the states of Tabasco and Veracruz. Later and further to the south in the Yucatán Peninsula, the Maya civilization flourished. They constructed cities in the midst of the jungle, complete with huge temples, courts in which ball games were played, and highly accurate calendars intricately carved in stone pillars. For some mysterious reason, the Mayans abandoned most of these great centers 1,100 years ago.

The Toltecs, in central Mexico, were the next major civilization. They were followed by the Aztecs. It was the Aztecs who built the city of Tenochitlán in the middle of a lake in what is now Mexico City, with long causeways connecting it to the mainland. By the early 1500s it was one of the largest cities anywhere, with perhaps 200,000 inhabitants.

Then the Spanish came. In 1519, twenty-seven years after Columbus arrived in the Americas, Hernán Cortés landed in Yucatán with just 600 soldiers plus a few cannons and horses. They marched inland, gaining allies as they went along among indigenous peoples who resented being ruled by the Aztecs. Within two years Cortés and the Spaniards ruled Mexico. They had conquered the Aztec Empire and devastated their great capital.

It was in that destruction that modern Mexico was born. The influence of the Aztecs and other indigenous people did not disappear even though untold numbers were killed. But neither can Mexico be recognized today without the Spanish influence.

Spain ruled for three centuries. Then in 1810 Mexicans began a struggle for independence from colonial Spain, much like the United States had fought for its own independence from Great Britain. In 1821 Mexico finally became an independent nation.

The newly born republic faced many difficulties. There was much poverty, especially among descendants of indigenous peoples; most of the wealth and political power was in the hands of a small elite of Spanish ancestry. To make things worse, Mexico lost almost half of its territory to the United States in a war that lasted from 1846 to 1848. Many still resent the loss of territory, which accounts for lingering anti-American sentiments among some Mexicans. The country was later occupied by France, but under national hero Benito Juárez Mexico regained its independence in 1867.

The next turning point in Mexican history came in 1911, when a revolution meant to help the millions of Mexicans stuck in poverty began against dictator Porfirio Díaz. There was violence and fighting until 1929, when Plutarco Elías Calles founded what was to become the *Partido Revolucionario Institucional*. It brought stability as well as economic progress. Yet millions of Mexicans remained in poverty, and as time went on PRI rulers became increasingly corrupt.

It was the desire of the people of Mexico to trust someone other than the candidate of PRI that resulted in the election of Fox. And so this nation of more than 100 million, with its ancient heritage, its diverse mestizo culture, its grinding poverty, and its glorious arts, stands on the brink of a new era. Modern Mexico is seeking a place as the leader of all Latin America, an ally of the United States, and an important voice in global politics. For that to happen, Mexico must narrow the gap between the rich and poor and bring more people in the middle class. It will be interesting to watch as Fox and the Mexican people work to bring their country into the first rank of nations.

A group of girls holding vibrant banners march in a Cinco de Mayo parade. The festival, held on the fifth of May, is one of the most joyful and widely celebrated of the year.

FIVE THOUSAND FIESTAS:
A PARTY EVERY DAY

According to the Mexican Department of Tourism, between 5,000 and 6,000 recognized fiestas (holiday celebrations) are celebrated in Mexico every year. These celebrations are religious, national, local, personal, and food related. On any given day of the year in Mexico, at least one fiesta is being celebrated somewhere in the nation.

Fiestas keep alive the traditions of various individual towns, cities, and states within Mexico. Fiestas also commemorate the important historical anniversaries of the United Mexican States. They pay homage to the special foods and crops of the nation, and they are held for birthdays, baptisms, weddings, and graduations. Some fiestas are thrown to welcome special guests to a town or to a private residence. Mexican postal workers even have their very own fiesta day!

Almost every fiesta in Mexico features special food, music, dancing, arts and crafts, parades, fireworks, parties, and prayer. Some of these celebrations have their own brightly colored costumes. Fiestas may be held in churches, town centers, private clubs, or personal homes.

Oftentimes, though, fiestas are held in the village plaza. Plazas are parks that are generally found in the center of a Mexican city, village, or town. Some plazas are paved with flagstones and lined with benches. Most are filled with beautiful flowers and lovely shade trees.

Piñatas are often hung from the plaza trees during fiestas. The village children take turns trying to break open these bright, candy-filled papier-mâché sculptures. When the piñatas break, the children scramble quickly to gather up as many goodies as they can.

Mexicans celebrate the major Catholic holy days of Christmas, Easter, and All Saint's Day. Christmas is celebrated differently in Mexico than it is in the United States, however. Mexicans exchange gifts on January 6, or the Day of the Wise Men.

According to Catholic tradition, every day of the year is dedicated to a different saint. These are the days that each saint

On October 12, Mexicans celebrate the Day of the Races. This day honors all the ethnic groups that have united to form the proud population of Mexico. Mexicans who are a mixture of Indian and Spanish blood are referred to as *mestizos. Criollo* is the Mexican name given to Europeans, Americans, and Canadians living in Mexico. *Mulattos* are a mixture of African slaves, who were brought over to Mexico in the 17th and 18th centuries, with Native Americans or mestizos. Native Mexicans are the direct descendents of the Aztecs, Maya, Olmecs, and other indigenous peoples of Mexico.

receives special honor and recognition from Catholics around the world. When the Spaniards came to Mexico during the 16th century, they brought with them the practice of celebrating a person's saint's day. Today, the individual saint's days are as important as birthdays in most Mexican homes. Each individual is honored and celebrated along with his or her saint.

People in Mexico love to celebrate fiestas. Entire villages get together to parade, party, and dance. The entire village or town often seems like one big happy family.

Some historians speculate that the reason Mexicans have so many fiestas is because they need to constantly cheer themselves up. Mexico's history is filled with hardship—conquering invaders, revolutions, poverty, and political turmoil. Mexicans may have a "live for today, for who knows what tomorrow may bring" attitude.

Mexican women wear brilliant, colorful clothing for many celebrations. Fiesta dress often includes exotic ornamental hairpieces and flowing skirts.

But another, more positive explanation for the number of Mexican fiestas is that these celebrations are simply displays of Mexicans' fierce

The Day of the Three Kings is an important element of the Mexican Christmas calendar. Festival-goers wear not only traditional fiesta dress, but also dress as the three kings and other Biblical characters. They develop costumes that include masks and props.

patriotism. The people of this nation feel intense pride in their past, their religion, and their complex ethnic background. For instance, Mexico has a nationwide celebration called the Day of the Races that celebrates ethnic diversity. Another fiesta day, Cinco de Mayo, celebrates the victory of the Mexican army over the French army at the battle of Puebla on May 5, 1862.

When the Spanish *conquistadors* landed in what is now Mexico, they encountered natives practicing a ritual called the Day of the Dead. In an attempt to Christianize this ritual, the Spaniards moved the fiesta from the ninth month of the Aztec calendar, usually the month

Rows of decorative masks line a table at a Mexican market. Folk art is a creative and profitable way to spread the Mexican culture.

of August, to coincided with the Catholic holy days of All Saints' Day and All Souls' Day (November 1 and 2).

The Day of the Races, Cinco de Mayo, and the Day of the Dead are all examples of the different kinds of fiestas celebrated by Mexicans. Fiestas are a means for Mexican families to honor their ancestors and share their memories and traditions with their children. Fiestas are an important joyous element of Mexico's colorful culture.

MEXICO'S NATIONAL HOLIDAYS

VIVA MÉXICO!

The government of Mexico recognizes a select group of national holidays by giving all Mexicans these days off from work. Schools are closed, and the post office, banks, and many other businesses close as well.

January 1 is the fiesta of El Año Nuevo, or New Year's Day. On El Año Nuevo, newly elected officials usually take office. The swearing-in ceremonies are often part of the fiestas. This holiday coincides with the Catholic observance of the Solemnity of the Virgin Mary.

February 5 is Mexico's Constitution Day. Mexico has had six constitutions during its history. The constitutions of 1857 and 1917

September 15 is a joyfully anticipated day in Mexico, as the nation celebrates its independence from Spain. Mexico became independent in 1821. Cities across Mexico set off glittering fireworks as part of the celebration.

were each passed on February 5. The holiday celebrations on this day are marked by official speeches across the nation.

Flag Day is February 24 in Mexico. February 24, 1821, was the date Mexico's War of Independence officially ended and independence was proclaimed. Mexico has celebrated Flag Day every year since 1937. On Flag Day, the people hold great celebrations in front of the memorial statute of General Vicente Guerrero, the first Mexican soldier to swear allegiance to the flag.

General Ignacio Zaragoza and the Mexican army beat the French in the battle of Puebla on May 5, 1862, even though the French were better equipped and had a much larger army. This battle took place after Emperor Napoleon III of France ordered French troops to conquer Mexico.

After the battle of Puebla, the French gained control of Mexico City. Napoleon established a French-backed government there. In 1866 and 1867, France withdrew its troops from Mexico because of opposition from many Mexicans and the insistence of the United States government.

March 5 kicks off Carnaval, an official Mexican holiday that consists of a five-day celebration before **Lent**. Beginning on the weekend before Lent, Carnaval is a time for parades, floats, costumes, music, dancing, drinking, and eating. Many people wear costumes and masks, while they dance and walk in parades.

In the evenings during Carnaval fireworks are set off using a traditional *castillo*, or castle (a large fireworks stage). Saturday evening during Carnaval, Mexicans enjoy the coronation of the Carnaval Queen and the silly Ugly King. The *Quema de Mal Humor*, or the burning of bad humor, sets fire to a dummy made to look like some unpopular character.

On Sunday, the biggest parades and

A Mexican women holds her daughter as they await a doctor's examination. Mother's Day in Mexico celebrates the sacrifices many mothers make for their children's well-being.

THE FESTIVALS OF MEXICO

fireworks are held. The people dance in the streets. Parents and children stay out together until late in the evening.

Monday brings the Day of the Oppressed Husband. Husbands are allowed to do anything they want, as long as it is legal and moral. They are given 23.5 hours of freedom on this day.

Finally, Fat Tuesday arrives. The people enjoy one last feast while they prepare to go back to work. They ready themselves for the spiritual sacrifices they will make during Lent. They arrange to attend mass the next day. Lent starts on the following day with the respectful celebration of Ash Wednesday.

March 21 is another national holiday in Mexico. It marks the nation-wide celebration of the birthday of Benito Juárez. Benito Juárez was a Zapotec Indian born in Guelatao, Oaxaca. Benito became the governor of Oaxaca, and went on to become one of the most beloved presidents of Mexico.

This fiesta lasts for six days in Guelato, Oaxaca. The president of Mexico and the Oaxacan governor visit the town on Benito's birthday. A civil-military

This statue of Father Miguel Hidalgo stands in the middle of a village plaza. Following Mexico's Independence Day, this statue will be adorned with red, white, and green flowers to acknowledge Hidalgo's influence in the fight for a free Mexico.

celebration is held that day. The other five days are filled with folklore, food, fireworks, and dances.

Yet another holiday occurs on May 1. This is Labor Day, or Workers' Day, in Mexico. Since this is a legal holiday, almost all businesses are closed. The workers of Mexico parade in the streets of their towns, villages, and cities.

One of Mexico's best-known fiestas is held on May 5. This holiday is known simply as *Cinco de Mayo*, which literally means the fifth of May. This fiesta is the celebration of Mexico's victory over the French army at Puebla in 1862.

Some residents of Puebla and Mexico City reenact the great Mexican victory at the battle of Puebla. Many Mexican cities are decorated with ribbons and flags. Military parades are held throughout the nation. Mexican school children practice with their school bands for months in advance, so that their schools may march in the Cinco de Mayo parades. Cheers of *"Viva México!"* are heard throughout the streets of the nation.

May 10 is a national holiday that has more to do with families than with history. On this day, Mexicans celebrate Mother's Day. The fiesta is particularly important since mothers are held in high regard in this culture. Mexicans honor mothers with gifts, serenades, and *mariachi* bands. To show their love and respect for their mothers many children sing the traditional song, "A Ti" (to you) to their mothers. They give their mothers candy,

The Mexican Flag is primarily three colors: green, white, and red. The green symbolizes independence; white symbolizes religion; and the red symbolizes union. Green, white, and red are used to decorate plazas, churches, public buildings, and homes for the Mexican Independence Day fiesta.

An important leader in the Mexican Independence Movement was a priest named Father Miguel Hidalgo. Hidalgo lived in Dolores, Mexico. He was planning a revolt for late fall of 1810.

The Spanish officials found out about Father Hidalgo's plans for a revolt. The Spanish government ordered the arrest of Hidalgo and his officers. The freedom fighter priest heard about this and rang the church bell on the night of September 15, 1910 to call his people to the church for a mass. When the church was full, Father Hidalgo encouraged the people to fight. He gave a speech that is now called the Grito de Delores. Father Hidalgo ended his speech with the cheers, "Viva México!" and "Viva la independencia!" These famous words are remembered and shouted each year on Independence Day.

perfume, clothing, jewelry, or flowers. During the evening, entire families gather and *serenade* mothers.

September 16, however, is another historical fiesta. Mexican Independence Day is a more important holiday than Cinco de Mayo for most Mexicans. Independence Day commemorates the beginning of Mexico's war of independence from Spain. The celebrating begins on September 15 when crowds of people gather in the plazas or *zocalos* (town meeting places) of their hometowns. The city center in Mexico City is decorated with red, white, and green flags, flowers, and lights. Vendors sell red, white and green confetti, whistles, horns, papier-mâché helmets, and toys.

At 11 o'clock, crowds all across Mexico grow silent. On the last strike of the hour, the Mexican president steps out onto his palace balcony. He rings a historic bell that was used by Father Hidalgo of Delores. He then gives the traditional speech called the *Grito de Delores* (cry of pain). After his speech, the president yells, "*Viva México! Viva la independencia!*"

Carnaval stretches over five days, encompassing Mexico's celebration of the traditional holidays before Lent. Festival-goers dress up and parade for Fat Tuesday and Ash Wednesday, as well as lesser-known days such as the Day of the Oppressed Husband.

Ernesto Zedillo, president of Mexico when this photograph was taken on May 1, 1999, waves to crowds during a Labor Day parade. With him are the Interior Minister Francisco Labastida (left) and the leader of the Workers Confederation of Mexico, Leonardo Rodriguez (right). Labor Day celebrates the industrious workers of the country.

People all across Mexico respond by yelling the same phrases. As they do, the air fills with fireworks, confetti, streamers, and cheers. The night sky is lit up with red, white, and green.

On the following day, September 16, statues of Father Hidalgo are decorated with red, green, and white flowers. People attend rodeos, parades, bullfights, and horseback performances. In smaller villages, cockfights may be held.

Columbus Day, October 12, is another important Mexican fiesta. Mexicans refer to this day as the Day of the Races. Although it is recognized as a national holiday, most businesses and government offices remain open. Children are given the day off from school, however.

The Day of the Races acknowledges Columbus's role in joining the Spanish people of Europe with the native people of Mexico. This day celebrates the mixture of the Old and New Worlds more than it honors Columbus. Not surprisingly, many Mexicans have mixed feelings about Columbus; after all, his arrival into the world of their ancestors was the beginning of years of foreign control.

After Columbus Day, come two important political holidays in November. On the first day of November, the president of Mexico gives his State of the Union Address. This coincides with the Catholic All Saints' Day. Then, on the 20th of November, Mexicans celebrate the anniversary of the Mexican Revolution of 1910. Parades, speeches, and other patriotic demonstrations commemorate the start of the war that overthrew the dictator Porfirio Díaz.

The Mexican National Holiday year ends with the celebration of Christmas on December 25. Children do not receive gifts. Instead, Mexican Catholics honor the birth of Jesus Christ on this day. Christmas is a day for mass, reverence, family togetherness, and prayer. Although Christmas is not a political holiday, because Mexico has so many Catholics and Christians Christmas Day is recognized as a national holiday.

Young girls hold candles as part of a procession during Holy Week before Easter. These processions are part of a tradition dating back to the time of Hernán Cortés's conquest.

RELIGIOUS OBSERVANCES:
PIÑATAS AND POSADAS

The religious observations of Mexico reflect the Mexican public's passionate devotion to the Catholic Church. As early as the 16th century, Spanish *friars* were sent to Mexico to convert the native people there to Catholicism. Sensing the Indians' love of ritual and ceremonies, the friars taught the native Mexicans about the Bible by using dances, plays, costumes, and masks to dramatize its stories. These practices are still evident in many religious celebrations throughout Mexico today.

Mexicans celebrate a great many religious holidays. Some of the more important ones are:

- Epiphany or Three Kings' Day, "Día de Reyes," in January
- San Antonio Abad or the Blessing of the Animals, also in January
- St. Valentine's Day in February

- Holy Week, in March or April
- "Santa Cruz" in May
- "Chalma" Lord in July
- San Francisco in October
- Virgin of Guadalupe in December
- "Los Posados" or the Nine Days of Fiesta, which include Christmas, in December

Many of these holidays are celebrated all over Latin America.

Three Kings' Day is a traditional Catholic holiday. Mexicans exchange Christmas presents on this day. They celebrate the gifts the three wise men brought to the baby Jesus.

The children of Mexico write letters to the three magi on January fifth. They place the letters in their shoes. Next, they put nativity scenes outside their homes. They also leave hay and water for the three kings' camels. In the morning, the children awaken to find their gifts left near the nativity scenes.

The story of chocolate begins in Mexico. A legend says that Quetzalcoatl, the god of light, descended upon the Toltecs of Mexico. As a gift, he gave the people the mystical cacao tree. In 1519, Spanish explorer Hernán Cortés tasted xocoatl, a chocolate drink made from the cacao bean. Cortez took the beans back to Spain. Chocolate soon became a sought-after delicacy throughout Europe.

Mexican bakers prepare delicious circular cakes for this day. The cakes are called the Rings of the Wise Men. A tiny porcelain doll is baked into each cake. The doll represents the baby Jesus and the gifts of the magi. The person who gets the slice of cake with the doll in it must throw another

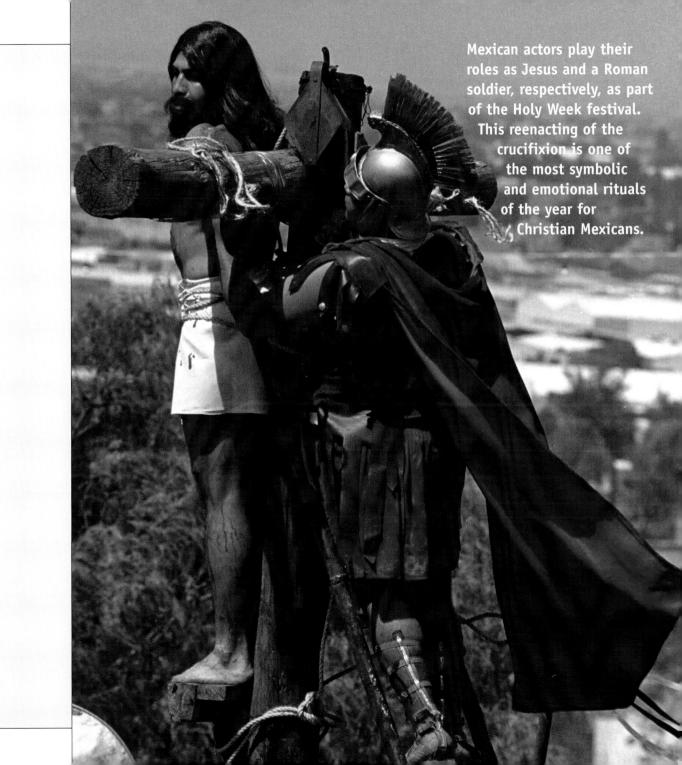

Mexican actors play their roles as Jesus and a Roman soldier, respectively, as part of the Holy Week festival. This reenacting of the crucifixion is one of the most symbolic and emotional rituals of the year for Christian Mexicans.

An actor playing Jesus Christ carries a cross through the streets of Iztapalapa, Mexico. Thousands of tourists flood the town each year to see the events of Good Friday reenacted.

party on February 2, or Candlemas.

On St. Anthony's Feast Day, a blessing of animals takes place in the Catholic churches of Mexico, since St. Anthony is the patron saint of domesticated animals. Many native Mexican cultures believed that animals had mystical powers, so this holy day was easy for the early Mexicans to accept into their culture.

Pets and livestock are decorated with flowers, colored streamers, and ribbons for St. Anthony's Day. Many people parade their chickens, horses, dogs, cats, and other animals around their towns. The animals are taken to church and blessed by a Catholic priest.

On St. Valentine's Day, Mexicans acknowledge the importance of love and friendship in their lives. Balloon vendors sell colorful, heart-shaped declarations of love in the streets. Chocolates and cards are sold in the stores and street markets. Young men stay up late into the night serenading their girlfriends.

Holy Week, the week before Easter Sunday, is time of prayer all over Mexico. Taxco hosts a world-famous religious festival between Palm Sunday and Easter. Thousands of **pilgrims** and **penitents** participate in the reenactments of the crucifixion of Christ.

Many towns prepare all year long for this week. They stage grand reenactments of Christ's Last Supper, Betrayal, and Judgment; the Procession of the 12 Stations of the Cross; the Crucifixion; and finally, the Resurrection. On Good Friday and Easter Sunday, churches are filled with those attending mass. Flower decorations and palm crosses can be found everywhere. Each community celebrates the holiday in its own way, but one tradition that is popular throughout the whole country is the breaking of *cascarones* (colored eggshells filled with confetti) over the heads of friends and family.

The Saturday before Easter, Mexicans participate in a ritual called "The Burning of Judas." (Judas was the apostle who is said to have betrayed Jesus Christ.) Mexicans burn cardboard likenesses of Judas. Some use this night to protest social and

On May 3, Holy Cross Day, Mexicans honor masons. The tradition began at the start of the Spanish colonial period in Mexico, when the churches were still being built. On Holy Cross Day, the priests would ask the masons to make crosses to place on the churches' highest peaks. The masons would climb atop the churches to secure the crosses there.

The bosses of Mexican masons still honor them on this day by letting them take long lunches. Some bosses even bring their masons food and beer. Masons and their families always have a special dinner at home to celebrate this day.

After the Lady of Guadalupe, an Aztec embodiment of the Virgin Mary, spoke to Juan Diego in the Aztec language, Diego told the local bishop that the Virgin had requested that a church be built on Tepeyac Hill outside Mexico City. The bishop did not believe him. He asked Juan Diego to provide him with some sort of proof.

The Lady of Guadalupe appeared again and told Juan to gather roses that had suddenly appeared on the snow-covered ground. He gathered the roses, and wrapped them inside his mantle. Then Juan Diego brought the roses to the bishop.

The bishop was amazed. Not only had Juan Diego brought him roses in the winter, but on Juan Diego's mantle was an image of the Virgin! The bishop now believed that Juan's visions were real. The Virgin appeared to Juan Diego two more times. In 1593 Bishop Zumarraga had the church built that Juan Diego had requested for the Virgin Mary. The mantle was enshrined in the church. In 1754 Pope Benedict XIV issued a decree dedicating December 12th masses to "Our Lady of Guadalupe." Our Lady of Guadalupe was designated Patroness of Latin in 1910. Pope Pius XII declared her to be the Patroness of the Americas in 1945.

political problems by burning likenesses of people they consider to be modern-day bad guys or "Judases." Sometimes the Judas images are stuffed full of fireworks. This way, they not only burn; they blow up!

On Easter Sunday, Catholics attend mass and take Holy Communion in honor of the Resurrection of Jesus Christ. Festive crowds gather in every town plaza after these church services. Street vendors sell food, balloons, and toys. Children and adults get ready to return to school and work, as this day signals the end of their two-week vacations.

Mexican Catholics have a deep love for the mother of Jesus Christ, whom they call Our Lady of Guadalupe. December 12 is the day she is said to have appeared as an Aztec princess to Juan Diego in 1591. Pilgrimages to the

Basilica of the Madonna of Guadalupe in Mexico City, processions in cities all over the country, dance performances, and special masses all mark the celebrations on December 12.

Because the story says that Our Lady of Guadalupe spoke in the Aztec language to an Aztec man, she is particularly beloved by the Mexican people. On her special day, people bring roses to her church. The Catholics of Mexico, which make up about 90 percent of the total population, all honor her on this day.

Christmas in Mexico is also an important holiday season with deep-seated traditions. *Posada* is

The Virgin Mary holds special religious meaning to devout Christian Mexicans. She is often called Our Lady of Guadalupe, because she appeared to a Mexican man in Guadalupe in 1531. During parades in her honor, the image of Mary is carried through the streets to the church built where she is believed to have appeared.

A Mexican construction worker places a cross on the summit of a building still under construction on Holy Cross Day. This tradition dates back to the days of Spanish rule, when the king would approve construction projects with the placement of a cross.

a vital part of this celebration. It honors Mary and Joseph's cold and difficult journey from Nazareth to Bethlehem in search of shelter. Every night from December 16 through Christmas Eve, a get-together is held in someone's home. The people eat, drink, and enjoy each other's company. The children enjoy special candies and fruits. At twilight, all of the party guests gather outside the house.

A small child is chosen to be dressed as an angel and lead the procession. Other children, carrying images of Mary and Joseph, follow this angel. Following them are still more children dressed in special robes and costumes. Finally, at the end of the procession, are the adults and musicians.

Everyone sings and carries lit candles. They parade around their neighborhood streets, and then they stop at a chosen house to sing a traditional **litany**. In the song, Mary and Joseph request shelter for the night. The song ends when those waiting behind the closed door turn the procession away. The group then parades ahead to a second home where the scene is repeated. At the third stop, the pilgrims are told that there is no room in the *posada* (inn), but they are welcome to sleep in the stable. Now, the doors of the house are pushed open, and the beggars are welcomed inside.

After the religious processions, come fireworks, dancing, drinking, and singing. The children are given a piñata to break at the end of this evening. Posada piñatas are traditionally made in the shape of a star to remember the light that brought the three kings to the newborn Jesus.

When the Posada is about to end, every guest receives a small gift, or *aguinaldo*, which is usually a package containing cookies, dried and fresh fruit, and *colación* (assorted candies). On Christmas Eve, Posada ends with midnight mass at the village church.

After mass, the village begins their celebration of the birth of Jesus Christ. One very old Christmas tradition is for all of the Christians in the village to gather in front of a *nacimiento* (nativity scene) to sing *villancicos* (Christmas carols) to the newborn Christ child.

Christmas day is a day for church and quiet reflection in Mexico, a day for rest and family togetherness. Christmas is the last major religious holiday of the year.

The Day of the Dead celebrates the souls of friends and family members who have passed away. Traditions for this day include portraying the figure of death and visiting the graves of the deceased.

ANCIENT FESTIVALS: FLYING MEN AND SUGAR SKULLS

Festivals and holidays have been celebrated since ancient times. The earliest festivals were connected with offerings to the gods; some were also remembrances for the dead. Planting time and harvest time were other occasions for special ritual celebrations. Candlemas, Corpus Christi, and the Day of the Dead are three holidays whose roots and traditions go back to the Aztecs of *pre-Columbian* Mexico.

February 2 is Candlemas, the end of the Christmas season for most modern Mexicans. In today's Mexico, cities and towns revel and make merry on this day with parties, parades, and bullfights. The streets are decorated with lanterns. Whoever found a doll in the cake on Three Kings' Day must host a big Candlemas party. The holiday celebrates both the Day of the Blessing of the seeds or crops and the Catholic celebration of the day Mary took the baby Jesus to the temple. In Mexico's smaller towns and villages, paper dolls of *brujas* (witches) are placed in the fields and gardens, while many Mexicans also attend mass on this day, mixing superstition and religion. The brown brujas are believed to ward off evil spirits, and white brujas are said to attract good spirits.

In late March, the Return of the Sun Serpent (the spring *equinox*) is celebrated at Chichén-Itzá in the Yucatán Peninsula. Local residents host a large fiesta that features light and sound shows, music, and dancing. Thousands of Mexicans and tourists come here to watch for the afternoon shadow of the snake-god Kukulcan. The people watch as the sun lights up the layers of the El Castillo Pyramid, forming sunlit triangles on one side of El Castillo from the top to the bottom. As the sun rises in the sky, more and more triangles appear down the side of the pyramid. Eventually, the sunlight shines upon a large snake's head at the bottom of the pyramid. This snake is Kukulkan, the Mayan god known as the Feathered Serpent. The Maya believed Kukulkan traveled down from the heavens to carry wealth and good fortune.

Mexican Catholics celebrate the religious festival of Corpus Christi, or the body of Christ, 60 days after Easter Sunday. Like much of the Mexican population, this holiday has become *mestizo*; in other words, it is a mix of Native American and

The Aztecs planned their festivals over an 18-month year. Each month contained 20 days. This left the Aztecs with an extra five days that did not fit into any of their months. These extra five days were thought to be very dangerous days when evil spirits could do great harm to the people. The people generally did as little as possible during this time, preferring to hide from the evil spirits.

The celebration of Candlemas in February marks the end of the Christmas season in Mexico. Traditionally, costumed parades process through most towns.

Spanish. On Corpus Christ, Mexicans honor the religious holiday as well as a native tradition celebrating the first fruits of summer.

At this time of year, the dance of *Los Voladores* (the Flying Men) is most likely to take place all over Mexico. This dance is a 1500-year-old rite originally started by the Totanic people. The dance is believed to

40

The celebration of the spring equinox dates back hundreds of years. Today, thousands of tourists gather at El Castillo pyramid to experience the once-a-year event.

have begun at El Tejin, near Paplanta, Mexico. It spread throughout Mexico and into parts of Guatemala. A special square was even reserved for it in Tenochtitlán, the Aztec capital. Today, the dance is performed all over Mexico for tourists, but the Paplanta Totenac Voladores are still known as the best in the country.

Five men dressed in multicolored outfits perform the *Voladore* ceremony atop a wooden pole that's as high as 105 feet. Sometimes, the men wear costumes to make themselves look like brightly colored birds. Four of the men perch on a tiny platform, wrapping their legs with long ropes, which are attached to the pole. The four men are thought to represent the north, south, east, and west—or perhaps earth, wind, fire, and water. The fifth man dances at the center of the pole on a tiny platform, playing a reed flute and a small drum as he dances. The four men then fall backward into the air, swinging around the pole. Hanging upside down with arms out-stretched, they twirl back toward the ground. Each flyer circles the pole 13 times during his fall. Between the four, this makes a total of 52 revolutions, one for each week of the year. They stop just inches from the ground, then flip and land on their feet.

But Mexico's most famous fiesta, outside of Cinco de Mayo, falls on November 1 and 2. November 1 is All Saints Day, and the Day of the Dead is November 2. Although each day has religious significance for the Catholic Church, the Mexican celebrations are really throwbacks to pre-Columbian rituals.

The original rites of the Day of the Dead have been traced back to the festivities held during the Aztec month of Miccailhuitontli. The Aztecs offered these celebrations in honor of children and the dead. They held their celebrations in the summer, however.

Spanish friars and priests considered the Aztec festival to be *pagan* and sinful. The Catholics wanted to change the celebration. By moving the date of the Day of the Dead festivities, they were trying to Christianize them. The Spanish Catholics hoped that the

The Aztecs worshiped the corn and rain gods from February through March. Poles were erected and decorated with banners in their homes and temples. Children were carried into the mountains and sacrificed to the rain gods. Quetzalcoatl, the greatest of the Aztec gods, was asked to use his powers as a god of the wind to push the rains away.

Aztecs would replace their Day of the Dead practices with the Catholic rituals for All Saints' and All Souls' Days. Because of the priests' efforts, Mexicans now celebrate the Day of the Dead in November, instead of in the summer. The celebration has retained most of its Aztec flavor, however. It is a fiesta dedicated to the dead, a time to remember lost loved ones, but the fiesta is not a somber time. Instead, it is a celebration of life, as well as a time of homage to the dead.

Skull-shaped candies are sold in the streets. *Ofrendas;* or little shrines covered with offerings, are built to honor departed family members. Some Mexicans build altars that look like they belong in a Catholic church, while other Mexicans build the traditional native-type altars used by their ancestors. These altars are pyramid shaped with five levels. Each level represents a stage in the life cycle. The first level is birth. Life and death are the second and third stages. The fourth level represents the evolution and cleansing of the soul. The fifth and final level symbolizes a return to new life.

Yellow marigolds, or *cempazuchitls*, are placed on the shrines, as these were the Aztec's flower for the dead. Skeleton-shaped decorations hang in the windows of most homes and shops. Cemeteries are crowded with families, who clean and decorate the final resting places of their loved ones. Marigolds are also used to form paths to the altars. These paths are believed to guide the smallest dead back home. These small dead are the departed children of Mexican families. On altars for these *angelitos* (little angels), candies, milk, sweet **tamales**, and the traditional *pan de muerto* (bread of the dead) will be placed. The *angelitos* are thought to return before the other dead, on October 30 or

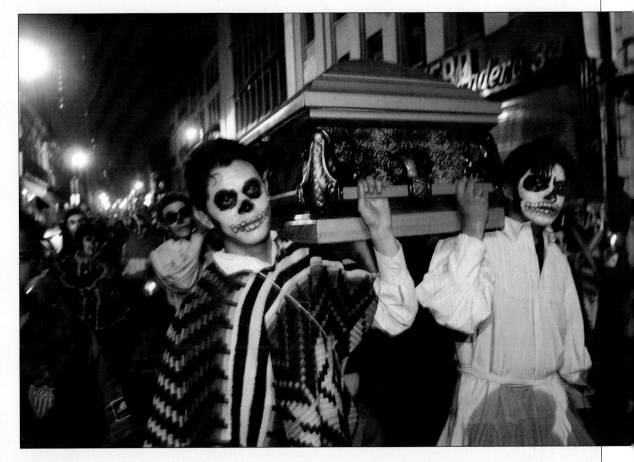

Townsfolk costumed as skeletons carry a coffin through the streets in a mock funeral. Celebrations for the Day of the Dead may appear morbid to outsiders, but they carry a great deal of significance for Mexican participants.

31. The families welcome the dead children with toys and other gifts. The *angelitos* then leave before the arrival of the other dead.

The altars for the adult dead, or the faithful dead as they are called, are made ready by the first of November. They are laden with offerings

A volador (flyer) hangs suspended from a rope. These men perform a pre-Columbian ritual that was intended to bring rain for crops. They jump head-first from a tall pole attached to a wound-up rope, which unwinds as they spin and fall to the ground.

such as *tequila*, tamales, **mole**, fruit, and *pan de muertos*. *Pan de muertos* is often formed into the shape of an oval, as many once believed that the spirit or soul is oval shaped. People also leave bread and water in corners of the local churches for those dead who have no remaining family to care for them. The graveyards are decorated with wreaths of orange and purple flowers. Bells ring in the arrival of the faithful dead. Candles are lit to guide the faithful dead back to their relatives' homes. A candle is lit for each lost soul, and the cemetery glows with the flames of hundreds of candles. Late into the evening, women pray for the dead, while the men sing and drink.

On the Day of the Dead, masked comedians, called *comparsas*, travel from home to home. Other actors and musicians often accompany them. Together, they make fun of the living.

On November 2, a special family feast is prepared. Again, *pan de muerto* is served. Like the doll in the bread for Three Kings' Day, a toy skeleton is often hidden in these loaves of bread. It is good luck to find the skeleton.

On the evening of November 2, people called **mummers** run around the town with masks on their faces. The mummers look for stubborn souls who refuse to return to the land of the dead. The mummers' job is to make sure that the stubborn souls go back where they belong.

After the mummers have chased away the stubborn dead, families begin to clean up. The altars are taken down. The skeleton decorations are put away. Life goes back to normal; the Day of the Dead is over until next year. The new year will bring a new cycle of ancient fiestas and celebrations.

Mexican weddings are a joyful affair, not only for the couple but also for the families and surrounding community. Traditionally, celebrations include Mexican food, music, and dancing.

LOCAL FESTIVALS, PERSONAL PARTIES, FOOD FIESTAS, AND FERIAS

Every village and almost every neighborhood of Mexico's larger towns and cities has a preferred saint (or patron) in whose honor local festivals are held once a year. These patron fiestas are often *novenarios*—nine-day celebrations. Patron saint *novenarios* are celebrated differently from place to place.

Personal parties include weddings, baptisms, First Communions, and Confirmation celebrations. Wedding anniversaries are also cause for large personal fiestas. Births and birthdays are celebrated as well.

In Mexico, the 15th birthday of a Catholic young woman is called her *Quincenera*, a very special celebration in her life. She will attend

A boy is blindfolded as he takes his turn at trying to break the piñata at a birthday party. The papier maché creations are hung from a string and usually contain candy and small toys.

a church service dressed in a fancy dress with five to seven maids of honor to attend her, just as a bride would have. She also has five to seven chambermaids.

The young woman's parents and godparents sit with her during the church service. The mass celebrates the fact that she has reached sexual maturity and is now of marriageable age. Often the masses will feature a long sermon on how a young woman of this age should behave.

After the mass, the chambermaids and maids of honor pass out small gifts called *bolos* to the guests. While the bolos are being passed out, the young woman takes her bouquet and offers it up to the Virgin Mary. Often, she will put her flowers at the

A traditional mariachi band fills a Mexican plaza with music. Mariachi bands are hired to play their cheerful music at restaurants and tourist spots, as well as festivals.

feet of a statue of the Virgin of Guadalupe.

Next, there is a party for the young woman. If she chooses not to have a party, she is also allowed to go on a trip instead, but most young women prefer to have a party. To reduce the financial burden, her parents ask her godparents and other friends to help sponsor this event.

The party will have plenty food and music. **Salsa** and mariachi tunes encourage lively dancing. However, the most important dance is a traditional waltz. The *festejada* (celebrant) and her favorite *chambelán* (escort) dance together to this song as the other partygoers look on. Then comes the customary toast. The festejada must also cut her birthday cake. The cake is made up of many layers and decorated to match the young woman's dress.

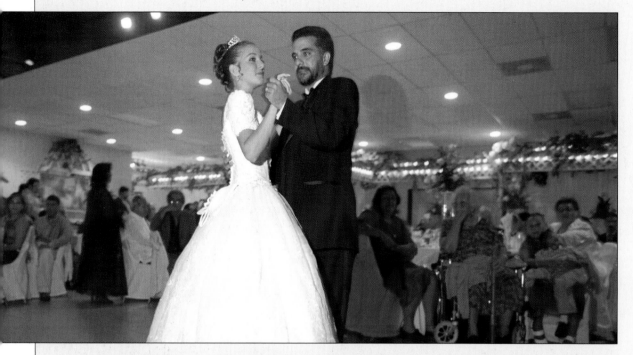

A young woman celebrating her 15th birthday dances with her father. This special day is called a quincenera, and marks the symbolic departure of a girl from adolescence to womanhood.

The celebration is a very important moment in the young woman's life. She is now allowed to date, and she is now eligible to marry.

Mexico also hosts a variety of food festivals and *ferias* (fairs) each year. A feria celebrates the local harvest. The food that is important to that area is featured and honored with samples of farmers' best wares. Dances, carnival rides, bullfights, fireworks, and food stalls add to the excitement.

Canelas, a city in Durango, hosts a coffee and ***guava*** fair from February 23 to February 26 of each year. Those who attend this food fair can try different kinds of local coffees. Guava juices, marmalades, and preserves are available to sample and purchase.

On March 11, the village of Dzula, a small *indigenous* village in Quintana Roo, puts on a traditional Mayan food fiesta. Their festival focuses on the foods of their ancestors, the Maya of the Yucatán Peninsula.

April is the month for Mexico's largest food fair, the Wine Festival in Aguascalientes. This festival lasts for half a month! There are many events to attend, including bullfights and cockfights.

Another food festival that lasts half a month is the Rice Festival in Escárcega, Campeche. It lasts from May 15 until May 31. Seafood and rice dishes are the main fare for this festival.

June 18 is the starting date for the famous Vanilla Festival in Papantla, Veracruz. Booths sell local food and beverage specialties. The flying *voladores* perform. The artisans sell small animal images and baskets woven from vanilla bean pods. Sachets and vanilla perfumes are also for sale. Paplanta is one of the world's largest vanilla producers.

From July 17 to 23 the Oaxaca Mescal Festival takes place. The people of Oaxaca build special wooden houses to display various blends of *mescal*. The Oaxacans are an artistic people, and they sell many arts and crafts at this fair, too.

August is the time for the Corn Festival

One baptism tradition that is practiced among some of Mexico's indigenous peoples is the placing of tiny farm hoes in the hands of the male children. The female children have small spindles for weaving cotton or wool placed in their hands. This is to honor the traditional roles as farmers and weavers that they will take on when they grow up.

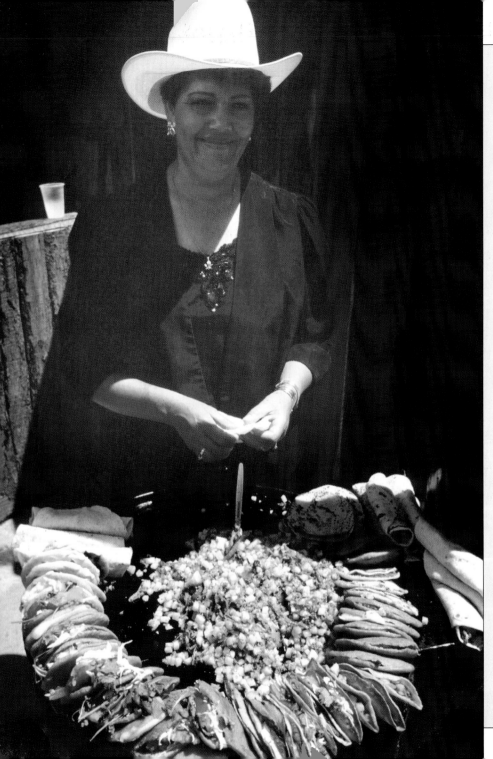

A vendor dishes out fajitas for hungry customers at a small food festival. Along with its music and customs, traditional cuisine helps to keep the Mexican culture thriving.

in Tala, Nayarit. This celebration probably dates back to the ancient Aztecs and their corn celebrations. Besides a great variety of corn dishes, the fiesta offers cockfights, bullfights, and dances.

September 14 to 16 are the dates for the Peach Fair in Sirutato, Sinaloa. Peach juice, preserves, and deserts are featured at this festival. Like at other festivals, the streets are filled with folk dancing and music.

On October 14 through 17, the Bread Fair takes place in Cholula, Puebla. The village constructs a giant brick oven in the town square. Bakers from the town of Cholula and other nearby villages and towns take turns demonstrating their skills at traditional Mexican bread baking.

On December 23, the people of the town of Oaxaca hold their radish festival. The radishes of Oaxaca grow to extraordinary lengths and often take very interesting shapes. Beautiful sculptures are made out of them, and a contest is held for the best radish sculpture. Entire nativity scenes are carved out of radishes! The people then have a parade with floats and music on Christmas Eve.

New Year's Eve marks the beginning of a fresh round of fiestas and festivals. The celebrations begin anew. Many visitors travel to Mexico just to witness one of these many fiestas.

CHRONOLOGY OF MAJOR MEXICAN FESTIVALS

Enero (January)
Month dedicated to the Holy Name of Jesus
   1 New Year's Day; Solemnity of the Virgin Mary
 2nd Sunday in January
     Baptism of the Lord
   6 Three Kings Day
  17 St. Anthony's Day for the Blessing of the Animals
  18 Santa Prisca, Patron Saint of Taxco
  20 St. Sebastian the Martyr

Febrero (February)
   2 Candlemas
   5 Constitution Day
12-14 Ajijic, Jalisco, Mexican National Chili Cook-off Championship
16-18 Xochimilco, D.F., Amaranth Festival
  14 Valentine's Day
23-26 Canelas, Durango, Coffee and Guava Fair
  24 Flag Day

Marzo (March)
Month dedicated to the worship of Saint Joseph
   8 St. John of God
  11 Dzula, Quintana Roo, Traditional Mayan Food Fiesta.
  17 St. Patrick, Patron Saint of San Patricio Melaque
  18 Nationalization of Petroleum Industry
  19 St. Joseph's Day
  21 Benito Juarez' Birth; spring equinox

Abril (April)

15-30 Aguascalientes Wine Festival

25 San Marcos, Patron Saint of Aguascalientes

29-30 Tlaxcalancingo, Puebla, Nopal Festival

30 Children's Day

Mayo (May)

Month of flowers consecrated to the Holy Virgin Mary

1 Labor Day; St. Joseph's Day

1-10 Rosario, Sinaloa, Regional Fruit, Vegetable and Salsa Festival

3 Holy Cross Day

5 Battle of Puebla, otherwise known as Cinco de Mayo

10 Mothers Day

15 St. Isador the Farmer, Blessing of Animals

15-31 Escárcega, Campeche, Rice Festival

20-28 Tequisquiapan, Queretaro, National Wine and Cheese Fair

22-30 Loma Bonita, Oaxaca, and Pineapple Festival

Junio (June)

Month dedicated to the worship of the Sacred Heart of Jesus

3 Corpus Christi

4 Pentecost

13 St. Anthony of Padua

18 Papantla, Veracruz, Vanilla Festival

3rd Sunday in June

Father's Day

24 St. John the Baptist

27 Our Lady of Perpetual Succor

29 St. Peter & St. Paul

Other spring holidays whose dates vary from year to year:
Carnival
Shrove (Fat) Tuesday
Good Friday
Easter

Julio (July)
Month of the Precious Blood of Christ
   4 Our Lady of Refuge
  16 Our Lady of Mount Carmel
17-23 Oaxaca Mescal Festival
18-25 Lunes del Cerro Festival, Oaxaca
  25 St. James the Apostle

Agosto (August)
   3 Ensenada, Baja California, Wine Grape Harvest Festival
  15 The Assumption of the Virgin Mary; Tala, Nayarit, Corn Festival
Aug. 20- Sept. 15
       Gomez Palacio, Durango, Cotton and Grape Fair
  28 St. Augustine, Patron Saint of Puebla

Septiembre (September)
Month of National Festivities
   1 President's State of the Union Address
  13 Young Heroes of Chapultepec
  14 Horseman's Day
14-16 Sirutato, Sinaloa, Peach Fair
  15 Independence Cry
  16 Independence Day
  24 Our Lady of Mercy
  29 St. Michael Archangel, Patron Saint of San Miguel Allende

56

Octubre (October)
Month dedicated to the Holy Rosary
1-12 Cuetzalan, Puebla, Coffee Fair
1-21 San Pedro Actópan, State of Mexico, Mole Festival
4 San Francisco de Asís, Patron Saint of Chapala
7 Our Lady of the Rosary
12 Columbus Day; Day of the Races; Pilgimage Guadalajara-Zapopan
14-17 Cholula, Puebla, Bread Fair.

Noviembre (November)
1-2 Day of the Dead
1-14 Chignahuapan, Puebla, Christmas Bread Fair
2 Day of the Dead; All Souls Day
12 Mailman's Day
20 Revolution Day
22 St. Cecilia, Patron Saint of Musicians
Nov. 28-Dec.28
  Gomez Farías, Tamaulipas, Corn Fair
30 St. Andrew, Patron Saint of Ajijic

Diciembre (December)
Month of the Nativity of the Lord and of the Virgin of Guadalupe
6 St. Nicholas
8 The Immaculate Conception
12 Nuestra Señora de Guadalupe (Our Lady of Guadalupe)
16-24 Pre-Christmas festivities
18 La Virgin of Soledad Festival, for the patron of Oaxaca
23 Oaxaca, Radish Festival
24 Christmas Eve
25 Christmas Day
28 Day of the Holy Innocents
31 New Year's Eve

GLOSSARY

Conquistadors	Spanish conquerors of the New World.
Equinox	One of the two times during the year when day and night are equal in length.
Friars	A special order of monks whose mission was to teach ordinary people.
Guava	A pear-shaped, sweet, yellow or pink fruit.
Indigenous	Native to a particular region.
Lent	The 40-day period from Ash Wednesday to Easter.
Litany	A repetitive chant.
Mariachi	A Mexican street band.
Mescal	A liquor from a Mexican cactus.
Molé	A spicy sauce made out of chilies and chocolate and usually served with meat.
Mummers	People who go merrymaking in disguises.
Pagan	Someone who has no religion.

Penitents	People who are sorry for their sins.
Pilgrims	People who leave their homes to travel for religious reasons.
Piñatas	Brightly colored, papier-mâché shapes containing candy and small toys.
Pre-Colombian	Before the arrival of Columbus in America.
Salsa	Latin-American music containing elements of rhythm and blues, jazz, and rock music.
Serenade	To sing outdoors at night to a woman.
Tamales	Ground meat seasoned with chili, rolled in cornmeal dough, wrapped in cornhusks, and steamed.
Tequila	A liquor made from the sap of a Mexican plant.

FURTHER READING

Baquedano, Elizabeth. *Eyewitness Books: Aztec, Inca, and Maya*. New York: Alfred A. Knopf, 1993.

Coe, Michael D. *Mexico, from the Olmecs to the Aztecs*. New York: Thames and Hudson, 1997.

Jermyn, Leslie. *Mexico*. Milwaukee: Gareth Stevens, 1998.

Johnston, Tony *The Day of the Dead*. New York: Harcourt, Brace and Company, 1997.

Linse, Barbara and Judd, Dick. *Fiesta! Mexico and Central America: A Global Awareness Program*. New York: Frank Schaffer Teacher Aids, 1993.

Rand McNally *Children's Atlas of Native Americans: Native Cultures of North and South America*. Chicago: Rand McNally, 1992.

Riding, Alan. *Distant Neighbors: A Portrait of the Mexicans*. New York: Vintage Books, 1989.

Stein, R. Conrad. *Mexico*. New York: Children's Press, 1998.

Winningham, Geoffrey, Richard Rodriguez, and J. M. G. LeClezio. *In the Eye of the Sun: Mexican Fiestas*. New York: Norton, 1996.

INTERNET RESOURCES

Discovering Mexico
http://www.nationalgeographic.com/mexico/

Mexican Heritage
http://www.angelfire.com/ca5/mexhistory/

Mexico Connect
http://www.mexconnect.com

Mexico for Kids
http://www.elbalero.gob.mx/pages_kids/geography/geography_kids.html

Mexico Online
http://www.mexonline.com/history.htm

Mexico People
http://www.theodora.com/wfb/mexico_people.html

Mexico Reference Desk
http://lanic.utexas.edu/la/Mexico

INDEX

PICTURE CREDITS

2::	IMS Communications, Ltd.
10:	Nik Wheeler/Corbis
13:	The Purcell Team/Corbis
14:	Robert Vander Hilst/Corbis
15:	Corbis Images
16:	Reuters NewsMedia Inc./Corbis
19:	Bettmann/Corbis
20:	Danny Lehman/Corbis
23:	Liba Taylor/Corbis
24:	AFP/Corbis
26:	Hulton/Archive
29:	Hulton/Archive
30:	Reuters NewMedia Inc./Corbis
33:	Fulvio Roiter/Corbis
34:	AFP/Corbis
36:	Sergio Dorantes/Corbis
39:	Nik Wheeler/Corbis
40:	Richard A. Cooke/Corbis
43:	Reuters NewsMedia Inc./Corbis
44:	Hulton/Archive
46:	Hulton/Archive
48:	Philip Gould/Corbis
49:	IMS Communications, Ltd.
50:	Hulton/Archive
53:	IMS Communications, Ltd.
Cover:	(front) IMS Communications, Ltd.
	(inset) Corbis Images
	(back) IMS Communications, Ltd.

63

CONTRIBUTORS

Roger E. Hernández is the most widely syndicated columnist writing on Hispanic issues in the United States. His weekly column, distributed by King Features, appears in some 40 newspapers across the country, including the *Washington Post*, *Los Angeles Daily News*, *Dallas Morning News*, *Arizona Republic*, *Rocky Mountain News* in Denver, *El Paso Times*, and *Hartford Courant*. He is also the author of *Cubans in America*, an illustrated history of the Cuban presence in what is now the United States, from the early colonists in 16th-century Florida to today's Castro-era exiles. The book was designed to accompany a PBS documentary of the same title.

Hernández's articles and essays have been published in the *New York Times*, *New Jersey Monthly*, *Reader's Digest*, and *Vista Magazine*; he is a frequent guest on television and radio political talk shows, and often travels the country to lecture on his topic of expertise. Currently, he is teaching journalism and English composition at the New Jersey Institute of Technology in Newark, where he holds the position of writer-in-residence. He is also a member of the adjunct faculty at Rutgers University.

Hernández left Cuba with his parents at the age of nine. After living in Spain for a year, the family settled in Union City, New Jersey, where Hernandez grew up. He attended Rutgers University, where he earned a BA in Journalism in 1977; after graduation, he worked in television news before moving to print journalism in 1983. He lives with his wife and two children in Upper Montclair, New Jersey.

Colleen Madonna Flood Williams resides in Soldotna, Alaska, with her husband, Paul R. Williams, and son Dillon Meehan. She is the author of an art unit for elementary students, entitled THE ANXIOUS ART TEACHER. She has been published in a variety of online and print publications. She is also the author of *The Geography of Mexico*, and *The People of Mexico*.